The Girlfriends Guide to Girl! Power

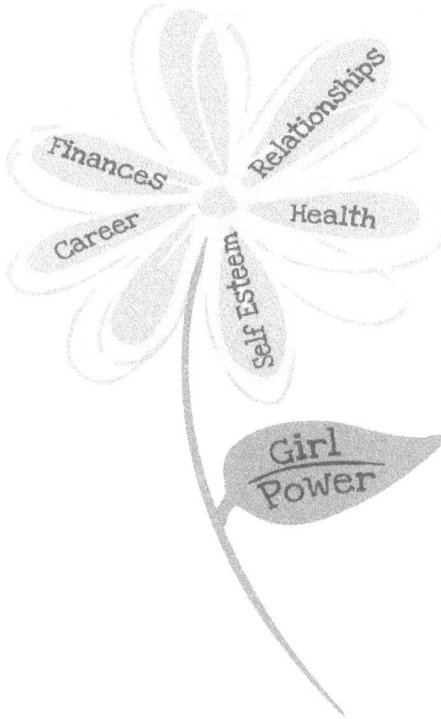

Finances
Relationships
Career
Health
Self Esteem

Girl
Power

Dawniel Patterson-Winningham

2nd Edition October 2011

Cover and Internal Design: HRD Design

Author Photo: Melissa Bliss/Shabby Chic Photography

For more information on increasing your Girl! Power or to share how girl power has changed your life, I would love for you to visit my web site at:
www.yourgirlpower.com

Follow me: www.twitter.com/yourgirlpower

On Face book
www.facebook.com/authordawnielpatterson winningham

DEDICATION

To my twins Hope and Faith, know that your mother loves you and wants the best for you always! Here is your instruction manual for *life*...

To all of the women who will love my son Tyler, here is your head start to happiness...

To all of the women I know and those I have not yet met, here is my gift to our generation and those to come. Use this information wisely...

Because I am a woman, I must make unusual efforts to succeed. If I fail, no one will say, "She doesn't have what it takes." They will say, "Women don't have what it takes." ~Clare Boothe Luce

10 RULES FOR BEING A GREAT GIRLFRIEND

1. I WILL RESPECT MY GIRLFRIENDS CHOICES, EVEN IF I DON'T FEEL THEY ARE RIGHT
2. I WILL ALWAYS GIVE MY HONEST OPINION IF MY GIRLFRIEND ASK
3. JEALOUSY AND EVNY WILL NEVER BE A GUEST IN OUR FRIENDSHIP
4. I WILL WORK TO FURTHER THE CAREERS OF MY GIRLFRIENDS AND THEY WILL DO THE SAME FOR ME
5. OUR RELATIONSHIPS WILL REMAIN POSITIVE AND WE WILL LIMIT OR ELIMINATE NEGATIVE CONVERSATIONS
6. WE WILL NOT TALK ABOUT OTHERS BECAUSE THIS IS A WASTE OF OUR TIME
7. WE WILL CONSTANTLY WORK TO GIVE BACK TO THE COMMUNITY AND TO THE WORLD
8. WE WILL STRENGTHEN OUR FAMILIES THROUGH POSITIVE ACTIONS
9. WE WILL UPLIFT AND SUPPORT OUR MEN AND ALLOW THEM TO LEAD WITH OUR SUPPORT
10. WE WILL LOVE OURSELVES WITHOUT MEASURE, WITHOUT COMPROMISE, AND WITHOUT FAIL

Table of Contents

Foreword
WHAT GIVES ME THE RIGHT?

The thing women have yet to learn is nobody gives you power. You just take it.~Roseanne Barr.

As a professional coach I encounter many, many women, and I always find myself lending advice about situations and issues that they face daily. As I work to coach them on business, inevitably there comes a point, sometimes very quickly, where business and personal meet. It is at that point that I find myself giving advice on both.

Let's face it. We are women. Our emotions guide us. If I am having problems at home, they impact my work. The faster I get over my problems at home, the better my work becomes. We carry our problems everywhere we go like a purse.

In my professional capacity I advise professionals on how to improve their relationships, performance, and persona. Naturally personal aspirations and challenges become a part of that conversation.

In short I have years and years of providing advice to women just like you. Old or young, it doesn't matter. It must be something in my eyes that says "Ask me!", and they do.

When it comes to me and my girlfriends, I am most often the one that has the most to say, right, wrong, or indifferent about how they should handle a particular situation.

Because I love to write, I thought to myself, let me get this on paper. We all need help, regardless of our station in life, or at least a different perspective on how to handle things.

Some of this you may know already. When you know better, you do better (sometimes! *smile*). Some of this may be a first for you. As the world changes, those life lessons that we have taken for granted have begun to be lost in translation... and in some cases, just lost.

This is an attempt to share some of what I was taught by Big Mama, my mama, my aunts, and a series of friends and acquaintances throughout the years. Share this book with your best friends, with your daughters and your sisters.

Donate a copy of this book to the library for the lost girl who doesn't have the support system she may need to be successful in this big, cold world. Start a Girl! Power group and make sure you and your crew stay grounded.

Most importantly, use this book yourself, even if you spend your head nodding every chapter, saying to yourself, "Dee is Crazy," or shaking your head and saying, "She is wrong for that." Sometimes my information may not be just the right thing for you, and that is fine.

With that being said, when you do finish this book, I challenge you to *do something*! If you feel the advice I am giving is not right for you, then I challenge you to figure out what *is* the right thing for. My feelings won't be hurt that you didn't take my advice (well slightly, but I will heal).

My motive behind this book is simple. In order for the world to be successful, we as women *must* be successful. Happiness for women is a must. We *must* love ourselves unconditionally. Girl! Power is what ensures the success of the Human Race. Without Girl! Power there is no future. As your power grows, so does the power of the women around you. The power that is needed to get this world back on track and to leave a better place for our children. It is up to us; Me and my new girlfriends (all of you). Bring along your girlfriends too and the other women in your life. The more the merrier. The more the powerful.

Now read on sister, and get ready to rock the world!

INTRODUCTION

HARNESSING YOUR GIRLFRIEND POWER

I do not wish them (women) to have power over men, but over themselves.~Mary Wollstonecraft

The road to success is paved with girlfriends. In saying that I don't mean that you are stepping over your girlfriends and other women to get where you are going. What I have experienced is quite the opposite. When we work together to support each others weaknesses and leverage each others strength we get to where we are going much faster. The obstacles that sometimes hold us back are minimized and in some cases eliminated.

This Girl! Power journey is proof that women are powerful within their own right. If and when you get a group of us together working towards the same or similar goals we are unstoppable. That means spending less time being messy and pointing out each others opportunities, and using our time to support our common goals and aspirations.

Take for instance our three most recent Nobel prize winners. These women Ellen Johnson-Sirleaf, Leymah Gbowee and Tawakkul Karman received the award for their non-violent struggle to end war in their respective countries Yemen and Liberia. One of the actions taken by Leymah Gbowee was to organize a sex strike with women across ethnic and religious lines. Let's stop there and reflect. This chick said, "Girl, I am tired of our men fighting these wars, are you?" For everyone that responded yes, her answer was "let's not have sex with ANY of these men until the war stops!" How powerful is that? This is only one of the many stories showing the power women have to accomplish great things by working together.

The women who won the peace prize worked within a nation to bring about change. Surely you can start the change within your own girlfriend group? There is no telling how far your impact will reach.

Share this book liberally with the women in your life. Spread the word like you would if your favorite shoe store is having a 50% off sale. Now I will admit that the business part of me says I wish you would each get your own copy! But the girlfriend side of me, the side that is your sister, says spread the word and to use my words to help each other with all of the love that was intended when I wrote them.

I believe in clear intentions so let me take a moment to tell you what this book is NOT. This book is *not* a manual. Meaning, this book is not a manual on how to keep your man, or how to get your man to love you, or even what to do if your man is cheating. This book is for *you and your girlfriends.*

Now that I have told you, and hopefully *after* you have already bought a copy of this book (*thank you Girl, I appreciate the love*) get ready to do some work on *you;* your goals, your dreams, and your future. This book is an opportunity for self improvement. I am a firm believer that only after you get *you* right, can you truly be ready for what life holds for you. I am no "Nostradamus". I am not even a member of the Physic Network (*but I love me some Dionne Warwick, hey girl*). However, experience has taught me that when you are ready for what God has planned for you, then you are in a much better position to hold on to it. Ask those million dollar lottery winners, who are now broke. They weren't ready. Will you be? Will you have the support needed to get you to the top and keep you there?

While you are working to improve yourself it is important to take those important women in your life with you; your aunts, cousins, daughters, co-workers, church members, and girlfriends. These are the women who were with you like four flats on a Cadillac when you were at a standstill. Now that you are gaining what it takes to be successful, what sense does it make to leave them behind? More importantly the journey to success is lonely. You need as much company and as much support on the trip as you can handle; and who are willing to come.

As I provide you with opinions along the way, you may not agree with me. You might even get mad or hurt. Sometimes our anger is the biggest influence for us to get up off our bountiful posteriors and *do something! Remember these are my opinions. Take the time to do your research and see what other opinions are available. Some opinions you may agree with more than mine. Other information may work better for you in your situation. The point is, do your research and know what works best for you.*

You may see yourself more than once throughout this book. As a matter of fact, the more bountiful your life (the more stuff you have to do) the more categories you will fit into.

You will also see other women in your life as you read through the chapters. Remember to share with them what you are learning. Allow them to read the book and take the time to discuss next steps. Keep the fire of growth going and be generous enough to see that although not all of this information will apply to you, it may apply to you later in life, or it may be relevant to someone around you now.

At the end of the book I encourage each one of you to chart your future based on your chosen types, and to complete exercises that will help you to see yourself in a happier, better place. Seek other resources on the subject of self improvement in order to add to the arsenal you will be able to access on the way to transforming your life. This book is a great start, but don't stop here. I once heard that if you read enough books on any subject, you become an expert. Seek to become an expert on you and improving your happiness.

Included will be ideas on how to add some Girl! Power to your gatherings. Any time you get together with your girls, you should spend at least 30 minutes to an hour discussing the positive. We spend that much time talking about what is on sale at Neman's, why not spend that much time talking about building success in our future.

Finally, please don't be offended by what you read. We all have faults, flaws, and issues. This is not meant to hurt you, but I have no choice but to be true to myself, and in doing so, I will be true to you. That's what a sister does, and I am your sister in this journey to loving yourself and tapping into your Girl! Power.

Truth forces change, so if you are not ready for change, you may not be ready for the truth. If you are ready for change, turn the page and get started. I already told you I am not tripping at this point, I did my part and wrote it down. *You* have to read it! *You* have to share it! It has to be important to *YOU*!

TO MY YOUNG GIRLFRIENDS....

The emotional, sexual, and psychological stereotyping of females begins when the doctor says, "It's a girl." ~Shirley Chisholm

Girls 12 – 21 (give or take)

If this is not you, then surely you know someone in this category. Take the time to pay forward all the seed that women have sown into you during your lifetime. This is the group that most needs our care.

If this is you, I love you and need you to love yourself. Always love yourself first and foremost; forever and for always. Compromising nothing for the love of you and what the future holds for you. You are unique, different, and beautiful just as God has created you. Hold on to that. Be on the lookout for more of the Girl! Power series created just for you. For now, read on, and be ready to take your place as the next leaders of the world.

Positive –

- ✓ You have your *whole* future ahead of you!

Opportunity –

- ✓ You are faced with many decisions that, if chosen incorrectly, could forever alter your path.

✓ Self Esteem can be a critical issue, impacting how you view yourself and therefore, impacting how you allow others to treat you.

HARNESSING YOUR YOUNG GIRL! POWER

This chapter (and this book actually), started as an open letter to my daughters Hope and Faith. They are currently 14, (going on 25) and I am constantly "advising" them on what to do, and what not to do. If this is you, or you bought a copy of this book for the young girl in your life, then take the time to read this part, let them read this part, or read this section together.

Baby, you are beautiful. You have your whole life ahead of you. I am not asking you to be perfect. I will love you in spite of your imperfections. I am asking you to be smart in the decisions you make that will impact your life forever. My mom used to forever say to me "think before you do". Now I am saying the same. Do nothing without first thinking, what does this say about me? How will this impact my future? Am I doing this because it is important to me, or to someone else? I love you baby! Now you must love yourself! And when we love ourselves, truly love ourselves; we must refuse to compromise who we are, and what we stand for. Think about the things that are important to you. Reflect on the things that make you happy. Give thanks daily for all that you have that makes you great. Now, refuse to compromise these things. Hang onto your conviction for dear life. YOUR life is worth it.

To tell a woman everything she may not do, is to tell her what she can do. ~Spanish Proverb

Drugs, Alcohol, and Tobacco All three of these have been made to seem glamorous by the media. The truth is, they are not pretty at all. All three of these put you on a sometimes irreversible road to death or illness. It is not worth the risk. If you partake in any of these, most times, you will be more willing to accept a mate who partakes in any of them and there you are stuck for life. You may change and they may choose not to. There are tales of girls who have smoked one cigarette, or done drugs once, had one drink, and as a result were killed without hope of a second chance. Or hooked, losing their hold on the future. Your chance starts now. Take the road less traveled and just say *nope!* Tell whoever offers either, that you love *you* much too much! If you have to tell them that Dee told you that you couldn't or shouldn't. Blame it on whoever you need to in order to resists. The choice is yours. Make the best choice.

Men While I will not sit here and blame the men of the world for our problems I will give you fair warning. Most men are fickle and rarely know what they want or what is in their best interest. Some fall in and out of love overnight and do what feels good at the time. Still others take forever to grow up. That being said, I am sure you will, at some point, run into a dude that you feel that you cannot live without. The question will be;

does he feel the same way about you? Want to check? Go a day or two without calling. Does he call you? Are you more into him, than he is you? Honest answers to these questions will lead you to the correct decision about your current relationship. Don't think that this is your last chance to interact with men. They will be there, and your future will too. Choose your future now! Choose YOU now!

Self Esteem If you don't do anything else that I suggest in this book, please take my advice love yourself. That is the one non-negotiable. If you can't love you, who will? You are different, but no less beautiful than the next girl; or the woman that's on TV. Don't beat yourself up, hate yourself, mistreat yourself, or lie to the world about who you are and the love that you have for yourself. Wear your love proudly on your sleeves. Do your best to take care of you and put your best foot forward. Start each day with a positive outlook and a great attitude. If things get bad, keep living. They will change. For the better or for the worse I can't promise you, but they will change. And that's life; it starts and ends with the love you have for you. I love you and you should love you too!

Don't take yourself too seriously. Make sure that your life is full of friends, hobbies, and interest to help you to occupy your time. This will provide you with the balance you need to ensure completeness in all areas of your life, and add to your happiness quotient. You are a young girl and you must live your life accordingly, free of many of the decisions and distractions that you will be forced to juggle as you mature. Have fun and avoid any situation that puts too much pressure on your ability to live your young girl life while you can.

Goal Setting I won't lie to you baby. Most of us spend our entire lives trying to decide what we want to be when we grow up. In the meantime, we have to do something to pay the bills. The key to being happy in your decision is finding out what you like to do, what you are good at, and what people will pay for. The combination of those three will equate to your career options.

Research any career that you came up with above. What schooling or experience does it take to get started? Based on your research, write down the seven steps it will take for you to reach for your goal. Give a deadline for each goal. By having your goals, actions, and deadlines in writing, it will help you to ensure you stray less from your path. Having a written plan gets you back on track more quickly if life throws you for a loop.

When you make your final choice (or choices) as to what you would like your future to look like, spend time each day visualizing the finished product. We can rarely bring into existence that which we cannot visualize. Create a dream board with pictures from a magazine that represent your future. Post it in a place where you can see it each day. You will be surprised as to how the universe will constantly offer up assistance to aid you in the journey towards your goal. You must first know where you are going.

Decision Making Many a good person was derailed by one bad decision. I know teenagers who went to jail when they were 17 and are still there in their thirties, because of a bad decision. When it comes to making decisions, don't make any decision that you would have trouble coming to grips with if the world were to change tomorrow.

If I could, I would provide you with a list of things you shouldn't ever do. Like don't ever get a tattoo of a man's name on you (I would prefer no tattoo's at all, but definitely not a man's name). Avoid being photographed with a drink in your hand. Absolutely never let any one video or photograph you naked. Be careful what you put on the internet... it stays there forever. The list could go on and on. But I digress. If I could only name three, they would be the big three listed above. But in the absence of those, I encourage you to think carefully about each and every decision as if it were the difference between life and death. It could very well be.

TO MY COLLEGE GIRLFRIENDS....

Women have been taught that, for us, the earth is flat, and that if we venture out, we will fall off the edge.
~Author Unknown

Girls currently attending college

If this is not you then surely you know a college girl. If so then pass this advice along to her. If you don't know any college girls maybe you should. This is a great opportunity to start a mentor relationship or reach out to a college girl in your area to support her physically and financially if you are able.

If this is you please know how very proud I am of you. There is a special edition of Girl! Power specifically for college girls that I am planning for you. For now please read and pay careful attention to the advice I give you here. Your education is the first step in determining how much the world will value you when you start your career.

Positive –

- ✓ You are laying the foundation for the career of your choice

Opportunity –

- ✓ A plan to get in and out of school with as little remaining expense as possible.

✓ Having career options lined up just in case "Plan A" does not work.

HARNESSING YOUR COLLEGE GIRL! POWER

If you have read the young girl section you are on your way to loving you, which is instrumental in the completion of everything else to come. Below are some recommendations for laying the foundation. You don't have to use them all, but experience tells us that the more we use, the better the chances of success.

Stay focused Don't let college partying and boys deter you from your study. There is plenty of time to play later, and trust that it is more fun when you have the money to play with and the career to back it up. If you feel the need for social interaction try creating study groups. This way you are working towards your goal while still being able to spend time with others.

Research your career choice With this ever-changing economy it is important that you are aware of the employment climate in your prospective career. Read and research job openings and salary ranges in your area, as well as other areas of the country, and know before graduation day, what your chances are of getting gainful employment.

Don't be afraid to be change your career choice if your prospective career choice is experiencing volatile conditions (ain't anybody *hiring in your field*) it is best you get out there early and make a change. There are books that will help you in the tasks of choosing your career change and help you brainstorm potentials close to your desired outcome. With a few course changes you are on your way.

Work for free This is advice I never thought I would give anyone, but experience, coupled with a degree, is worth much more than just a piece of paper. I would encourage you to find a paying internship, but if that fails, don't be afraid to seek out free summer internships. You will not only gain experience, but you will gain successful lifelong contacts in your field. Internships also give you a much needed "foot in the door" and access to contacts you may need later to find your dream job. Another benefit of working for free is that you get a chance to experience your career choice before making your final commitment. There is nothing more important than doing what you are passionate about. Being an apprentice or intern gives you a chance to see if your chosen profession is everything you thought it would be and more.

Network College is the perfect place to build contacts for now, and for later. Some of the college people I know don't pay full price for anything because they have built a network similar to a barter system in which their old classmates work together to get the best deals on everything from cars to houses. Make your degree and your contacts work for you.

Get a mentor Don't be afraid to tap into the professional community and find someone willing to take you under their wing. It will save you a lot of time, frustration, and wasted effort in the future. A mentoring relationship is something that you should work to continue throughout your life journey. Make sure your mentor is someone who has "been there, done that" and has something to offer you on your path to building a better you. You may outgrow mentors during your life journey, but never forget to recognize them for their contributions to your life, or forget that you will need to pay it forward with others as you start to rack up your professional accomplishments. Help someone else over the wall!

I have a college man Trust me, your college man would not be willing to put his career on hold for you, nor should you for him. If you love you, then push through. True love will wait and understand your need to get on with your studies. Also who says you can't have it all. True love will find a way to compromise without compromising your studies or your future. It may seem important to you now, but put yourself in a time machine and try to see 5 years from now, or 50 years from now. Will this relationship still be important? If so, it will stand the test of your studies. If not, it was not meant for you anyway.

Keeping up with the Jones' It is easy to allow credit to take you over, trying to keep up with the latest college fashion. 5th Avenue can wait until you have a great paying job. Learn to cultivate your style with a pair of jeans and some t-shirts that you can wear faithfully and push through. Refuse to allow credit to overtake you at this early age.

Is this my bill If you must go into debt for your college education, do your best to minimize it. Can you work on campus to get a reduction? Can you take classes at a community college and transfer to a major university when its time for graduation? Review your grant options before taking out low interest loans. If you spend the first five to ten years paying back your debt, is the degree worth it? What businesses can you start while in college, that will help you to finance your degree? There are books and internet articles written to help you get past this stage without becoming an indentured servant for the next seven years. Take advantage of the available information, do your research, and avoid debt if at all possible. Make wise decisions about your future.

I know this is a lot to digest, but I want to make sure you understand the risks. You have chosen a great path and I am proud of you. It is up to you to stay on your path to higher education.

Take the time to research each of the potential pitfalls and recommendations for laying the foundation. I encourage you to start with these points and document what you are doing to address each one.

Partner with the girls on your campus to start support groups that can help you address some of these challenges. There is power in numbers.

TO MY CAREER GIRLFRIENDS....

Give a woman a job and she grows balls. ~Jack Gelber

Any girl gainfully employed (need I say legally).

If this is not you, give extra respect for the women in your life who are out there hustling for their families. You are blessed to not have to endure this hustle, although I am sure you have your own set of issues.

If this is you know that I am right there with you. I do my best to provide for my family and our future. Read on and keep working towards being the best at what you do, and always doing what you love to do.

Positive –

- ✓ The fact that you have a job is definitely a positive

Opportunity –

- ✓ May have glass ceiling limitations or may have a position with limited future potential

- ✓ May be undervalued in your current role

- ✓ May be underpaid (and overworked)

HARNESSING YOUR CAREER GIRL! POWER

First, allow me to applaud you for taking the first step in spreading your wings. I was always taught that hard work was the key to success. Only after working three fast food jobs (at once) did I learn that there was more to it than that. Below are some tips to get you on the right career track and how to better tell when you are.

Do you love (or at least like) what you do If not, start to look for something else and don't stop until you find something you at least like. Many of us get caught up in the fact that we have a job at all, and it is only when we are laid off, fired, or downsized that we decide to look for something else. Don't wait, start looking now.

Seek help Make everyone you know aware of what you would like to do. If your circle only includes club friends then broaden your circle. Network like there is no tomorrow. People will hire someone they know with little experience, before they will hire someone they don't know. This is also true if you are trying to break through the corporate glass ceiling. You can't hide in your office and think the talent police will find you. Attend corporate events as if you belong there and network with the people who make the hiring decisions. You never know who you will meet later in the interview room.

Find a mentor You would be surprised at the number of women I have seen come to job interviews without being dressed professionally. My first mentor would send them away and reschedule them to come back, dressed professionally! The message about finding a mentor is this; it doesn't have to be the person with the biggest car or flashiest jewelry. It has to be someone who is willing to take a chance on you and make an investment in your personal improvement. They have to know far more than you and be willing to teach you what they know.

Can you make more working for you Many of us spend our entire adult lives working for someone else; waiting on a pay increase, or recognition that may never come. It takes initiative, planning, and bravery to strike out on your own. That doesn't mean quit the job you have now (You won't say I told you that). What it means is that you should start evaluating the things you are good at, and that you like to do, and incorporate those talents into a side line gig that could eventually grow into a full-time business. You have what it takes, but do you *have what it takes?*

Get hungry I think comfort is the number one pitfall. I used to be comfortable. Decent pay, decent benefits. I had to get hungry for the next level. Hungry to tell my story, help others, and yes, get paid for it. So if you are comfortable, throw complacency and get hungry.

You are your worst enemy In all of this, look for the 'you devil' on your shoulder who is telling you that you can't do it. You can't find another job, you can't strike out on your own, no-one will pay you for your talents. Tell that 'you devil' to go suck an egg and shut up. Every day wake up telling yourself that you can do this, another job is waiting on you, and that people will pay you for your ideas and/or talent. There are millions of people walking around in CROC shoes right now because someone couldn't be stopped.

Evaluate Do you like your job and want to move up? Do you need a career change? Can you strike out on your own, and if so, what service could you legally perform?

Make a plan What do you need to get started? Research? A mentor? More networking? A web page? Start-up capital?

Stick to the plan For each action you list, list a deadline and a reward. Enlist your close friends and family members to keep you on track. Hold yourself accountable to your career goals and your career happiness.

Get reinforcement to overcome the fear There are many books and internet articles to help you uncover what is holding you back. *You* are holding you back. I am just learning of the many tools available to help me keep pushing through and some days, trust me, I have to use them all to keep me pursuing my dream without fear.

It is one career all females have in common, whether we like it or not; being a woman. Sooner or later, we've got to work at it, no matter how many other careers we've had or wanted.-Jilly Cooper

TO MY MARRIED GIRLFRIENDS....

I, with a deeper instinct, choose a man who compels my strength, who makes enormous demands on me, who does not doubt my courage or my toughness, who does not believe me naïve or innocent, who has the courage to treat me like a woman. ~Anaïs Nin

Married Girls <u>(for the sake of argument, if you have been with your man more than a few years and you are cohabitating)</u>

If this is not you, be hesitant in the advice you give your girlfriends, and give advice only if they ask and are sincere in wanting to know the truth.

If this is you, allow me to say congratulations. Marriage to the right person is one of the most beautiful things that you can hope for in life. I hope that my words below are a help to you and your partner. Read on and keep the love alive.

Positive –

- ✓ Partnership and companionship to face the world

Opportunity –

- ✓ Self happiness
- ✓ Threat of break up

HARNESSING YOUR MARRIED GIRL! POWER

I definitely have the authority to write this section... been there, done that. Man didn't I learn a lot. More than I could have hoped to learn in a lifetime! Not just personally, but from the myriad of my girlfriends who have been there, are still there, or are on the way there. Every shoe I discuss will not fit you, and if it doesn't fit, then don't put it on, silly. But if it fits (however painful it is to admit it), quietly slip the shoe on, sit back, and listen. I told you before; this is not a male bashing book. I refuse to do it. This is all about you and your power. Get on board chick and get your power back.

Two heads are better than one If you are married, I applaud you. If you are *happily* married, you receive a standing ovation. You definitely have an advantage over the single world. Life is much easier if you have someone to get your back, and someone you can count on. Don't let silliness get in your way. Stay grounded and stay in love. Always date your man. Keep some mystery. Don't stop buying lingerie, or having date night. Keep meeting at home for "lunch" in the middle of the day, if you can. If you keep it fresh for him at home, you improve your happiness quotient and improve your chances of a faithful relationship.

Don't let money ruin your relationship Money will be there. Love may not. Never have your eggs in one basket. Keep a rainy day stash. If you saw the movie

'**Jump the Broom**', her husband lost all of their money in the stock market. It was not his fault, just a sign of the times. She had a rainy day stash equivalent to what he lost. It didn't mean that she loved him any less, or that she didn't trust him. It just meant that she had his back, *and* her own! That's what couples are for, right? We can't both be slipping! Plus, life is unpredictable. If life was to take an unexpected turn, the true test of continuance is; will you be able to make it without his income or without yours? Whether one of you is downsized, or one of you passes away unexpectedly, do the right thing to ensure continuity for your family.

Be honest about your relationship Honesty is the best policy. I used to think my relationship was good because he didn't smoke, drink, do drugs, gamble or any of the other taboo things. The truth was, we didn't get along; and we both stayed way too long. We said it was for the kids, but if we told the truth about it, it was just too hard to leave, split everything, and start over. I had to finally make the decision to be honest with myself. My happiness comes first. Are you really happy? Is there a chance that you can regain your former happiness?

Don't shy away from getting help. I have always envied those people who are quick to run to counselors and therapist. Today most of us have more resources available to do the same. If there is a shred of a chance for you to save your relationship, even if you have only little irritating problems, sometimes getting help will help you to get where you need to be before you hit rock bottom.

Be you! Being part of a team, it is easy for one to get lost in the shuffle. Just make sure it is not you. Keep your friends. Keep your career. Keep your family. Keep your bank account (real talk). Keep all of the things you had when you were single. You should never lose you to be part of a team. Failure to keep your own identity is what the old people call 'keeping all of your eggs in one basket'.

Improve you! My theme throughout this book is that we all have room to grow. Failure to improve you, to read and be exposed to the world, sets us up for failure. Keep moving to the next level and refuse to stay stagnant. I know personally I spent a great deal of time begging my man to move to the next level instead of moving on ahead and having faith that he would join. Greatness rubs off on people. In cases where it doesn't, you outgrow people. It's their choice. You make your choice when you choose to continue to improve yourself.

How well do you really know him I have seen, heard of, and witnessed first hand break-ups that appear out of the clear blue sky. You may be, on one hand, thinking things are good, and your mate is thinking something totally different. And keep in mind, things happen. Emergencies could leave you reeling... and alone. Be prepared, at least financially. Stephen King has a book, 'Full Dark, No Stars'. The woman is married for years and finds out her husband is a serial killer. You may think that's a stretch, but I have heard stories of women who find out their husbands are pedophiles, rapists, bank robbers, and other such madness. Trust your gut when it comes to your marriage. If you feel something is wrong, you are either right, or paranoid. At any rate it's worth further investigation, after all, this is your life.

I don't want to be alone Many girls (present company included), hate being alone. So we settle. We settle for dudes that don't make us important, that don't work around the house, or work at all in some cases. But remember, this book is about you. Tell yourself daily, I am loved, and I am in love. Doesn't mean you have to stay in your current relationship. You will, however, have to develop your self confidence in order to change your situation into something that improves your happiness quotient.

I'm here for the kids Many people (this was me too) use the kids as a crutch to stay together, even though they are miserable. Don't do it. Kids are remarkably resilient and this may sound cliché (but I am going to say it anyway), you will still be parents, even if you are not together. Those kids will be grown and gone, and you would have wasted part of your life being unhappy. Refuse to compromise. Don't misquote me, I am not saying, don't try to save your relationship. Salvaging a lengthy relationship is always the best course of action. Know when to cut your losses. Don't stay for the wrong reasons. If you don't love him, can't stand him or you don't get along, then change your situation; whether you have kids or not.

Keeping up with the Jones' My grandma used to say money was the root of all evil. She never told me it was the root of all marriages. It is the one thing that will really make you fall apart. So keep it in perspective. Live within your means. Don't try to buy a new car every few years because your friends do. And don't stay together because you are afraid of what people will say. Forget people! Choose to do what makes you happy without fear of what others may say.

Continuously evaluate the relationship. Cars get tune-ups, people get check-ups, why shouldn't your marriage? Communication is critical. There is only one form of communication that is fair, and that is direct, face to face communication. Sit down with your partner at least once a year and talk about where you are, and where you would like to take the relationship. Sort of like an annual review at work, or an annual report for a company. Doesn't this lifelong partnership deserve the same attention?

Be honest about the results. Whatever you decide as a result of the evaluation, make sure you are the priority of the outcome. If you are not the priority, go back to the drawing board until you come away with an outcome that is purely and selfishly about your happiness in the relationship.

Build a rainy day fund. And I don't mean a couple thousand dollars. You may need to start small, but think of the fund before you buy that next new car; Or before you make that next trip to the mall. Your rainy day fund should carry you and your family for six months minimum. This does not include the private fund that we discussed earlier. Don't think of it as a break-up fund. Think of it as a stay-together fund. You may just need that money to stay together one day. Ask some of the folks who are losing two incomes at a time. The past few years has taught us some valuable lessons. Let's not be so quick to forget them

Never let the hand you hold, hold you down. ~Author Unknown

To My Single Girlfriends....

I wish someone would have told me that, just because I'm a girl, I don't have to get married. ~Marlo Thomas

Single girls (includes separated, divorced, never married)

If this is not you encourage your single girlfriends and help them look for the positive in being single. Especially encourage those who may feel as if their biological clock is ticking. Let them know that God has someone planned for them; they just need to be patient to find their Boaz.

If this is you continue to work on you until you are at the level where meeting your right mate works for you. Don't compromise and don't rush. Read on and be empowered and encouraged.

Positive –

    ✓ Freedom to find and love you

Opportunity –

    ✓ Partnership and Companionship

    ✓ Finding a mate

Harnessing your Single Girl! Power

It may be because I am getting older (some say the older the berry, the sweeter the juice! Or is it blacker the berry? Oh well!), or it may be that I am getting wiser. At any rate I am finding power in living a single life. Not to say that I don't yearn for companionship (and that other stuff). I am just saying after years of having to bolster someone, hold someone's hand, consult with someone first, there is a renewed power in the ability to just be me!

Find yourself and love will follow I can't express to you enough that the most important person in the world is you. I am not saying that to be arrogant (although people may accuse you of such). I am saying it to be real. If you don't take care of you, then how could you possibly take care of someone else? At the same time, if you don't *love* you, then how could you love someone else? Being my best me, allows me to be the best for those around me. Don't put the cart before the horse and look for your soul mate. I speak from experience that if you are not on the road to being the person you want to be, then you will quickly outgrow the mate you choose.

Let the past be My big mama used to say, no sense crying over spilled milk. That's true for love lost. Life has a way of giving you what you need, when you need it. I am saying, don't cry over the past. I am not saying don't learn from it. If you continue to choose relationships that are not healthy, then it is you who must work to correct the choices you make. (Like the old people say... if it smells like cabbage and you move but the smell follows you. Then it's you). Look to yourself first and what kind of vibes you are sending to continue to attract the same relationships.

If you continue to meet guys that don't work out for you in clubs, then change your surroundings. You may be investing too much in relationships when they first start. Change by holding something back until time shows you the relationship is worth investing in.

Desperate for companionship You don't have to be. You can date, without sex and without commitment. Let it be your choice. You should collect jerseys (names and numbers) so that you have choices. Who is the best dinner companion? Who is the best companion for trips? You are single and you don't have to worry about how it looks to date. I do caution you about this new trend friend with benefits. As women we are emotional creatures and tend to create emotional ties. So if this guy calls you at 2am in the morning after he leaves the club, and doesn't commit to anything else with you during the week, ask yourself who is really benefitting?

Wrong choices I talked about wrong choices in men, but I also want you to be aware of other wrong choices. You may hear them already on TV commercials and on the news, but I would be remiss if I didn't tell you, it is a wrong choice to have unprotected sex. It is a wrong choice to have many sex partners. Protect your future, and protect your life. There is no such thing as 'he looks clean'. Remember this is all about you!

Clock ticking Don't allow the fact that all of your classmates or your girlfriends are getting married. For example, say I get married at twenty years old. Do I really have enough growth under my belt to say I will be with this man for the next eighty years? (Yes, I am living to be a hundred or more.) But if I wait until I am thirty, the chances of maturity are better. I am not saying, never get married early. I am saying make sure you make the right choice; a choice that will sustain the test of time. Mother Nature will wait. I had my first kid at twenty-five. There are women who are forty and having kids. Don't let having kids influence your decision to choose the wrong man, which will in turn lead to be the wrong father for your kids.

He's taken Don't fool yourself. If he is cheating on his lady, he will cheat on you with someone else. Many men will never leave the woman they are with for you. And if he did ever leave her, could you trust he wouldn't do the same to you? Besides, if you have this man in your life, you are not free for the man of your dreams to approach you. Get rid of that placeholder. You are only stopping God from sending you your very own soul mate.

Build your brand, don't build your man There are so many women who are defined by their man and their relationship. If you have your own brand and his just happens to be more popular than yours, then this is ok. Don't look for a man to define you. The closer you are to fulfilling your personal destiny, the better selection you will make in your mate. For example, when I was younger I used to go out almost every night. Meaning I would choose a man who went out every night and thought it was ok for me to go out every night also. What would happen when I grew out of that lifestyle and the man didn't? He would continue to go out every night, while I sat at home alone, mad because he didn't change when I did.

Be patient and make the right choices Think before you do anything. I know I am truly growing up because I say this more and more. Think about how what you do now, impacts you for the next year, the next five year, the next ten years and even the next fifty years. If the impacts are ok, then move forward. If you can't stomach the impacts for the next fifty years, then don't do it.

Don't give away free milk You know what I'm talking about. What's the saying? 'Why buy the cow, if you can get the milk for free?' That's as real as it gets. If you are already picking up his dry cleaning, cooking for him, paying his bills, and whatever else it takes to get him to think of you as wifely, then chances are he may not 'wife' you. Be honest to yourself about what you want out of the relationship. There is nothing wrong with cooking an occasional meal, but always remember you are single, and therefore you are dating. In all of nature, it is the role of the male to impress upon you his ability to take care of you as a mate for life. Don't relieve him of this responsibility to impress you.

I think, therefore I'm single. ~Lizz Winstead

TO MY DIVORCED GIRLFRIENDS....

I asked a Burmese why women, after centuries of following their men, now walk ahead. He said there were many unexploded land mines since the war.
~Robert Mueller

Divorced women (includes those who are separated or have broken up with a long term live in partner)

If this is not you, know that there are many emotional stages that come about after a divorce. Support your girlfriend while she is going through these emotions, but do not allow her to get bogged down with anger. This divorce may have been the best thing that ever happened to her. Keep reminding her that she needs to love herself, and regain who she was before she was married.

If this is you it is ok for you to be hurt and angry that this has happened. Remember God loves you and has a plan for you. Keep reading and continue to look for ways to move you out of the past and into the future.

Positive –

- ✓ Chance to start over and find you and your soul mate on the same journey

Opportunity –

- ✓ Self esteem

- ✓ Financial hardship

✓ Partnership or companionship

HARNESSING YOUR DIVORCED GIRL! POWER

Welcome to the divorced woman club. You got here one of two ways; either you got tired and left him, or he got tired, and left you. At any rate, you are here now. What's next?

Love you I want you to think really hard about loving you. So hard that you work to make sure loving you is a priority. That means start your day by saying I love you, Girl! Doesn't necessarily mean go to the mall every day and buy your love; that really doesn't work. Take care of yourself and love yourself first. Write down ten things you love about yourself. Then write down ten more. I would challenge you to even write down ten things you don't like about yourself and then work for thirty days to change them. That exercise will definitely show your commitment to self improvement. There is no love like love of self. If you already love you, then work to make sure the world knows it. There is a difference between arrogance and self love. Arrogance tends to hurt others, while self love is designed to improve and protect you.

Accept and move on It's no one's fault that you are no longer together. Whatever steps you need to accept it and move on, then do so. I am not saying that you will get over it immediately. Love hurts, and break-ups hurt worse. I am saying be proactive in your own recovery. I know women who have been divorced for years and find it is still a point of pain. Use this break up instead, as a stepping stone for your future. As women, we will encounter a lot of heartbreak and let-downs. What doesn't kill us damn sure makes us mad (and it makes us stronger too)! If you need to seek counseling or have a waiting to exhale party with your girlfriends to feel better, then do it. You may need to even go to Vegas and rip it up like paper. Do it. The point is, whenever you get to the point where you have talked about it all you can, accept it and move on. It's his loss; ask my ex! If you were his everything, like we tend to be, it won't be long before he realizes that he didn't just lose a wife. He lost a chauffer, accountant, cook, assistant, maid, and best friend. You get it. His loss! Your gain!

I will survive! (On one income) One of the reasons I stayed with my ex for so long was money. It was easy to say I stayed with him because the kids needed a father, but you bought this book, so I must keep it real. I stayed because that fool was getting a check. He knew that if at any point his checks stopped coming, then his lease (at least the one in my house) would be up. To keep it real, I eventually had to make a choice. Choices fall like dominos; you can't really make one without making another. I chose to be happy, which meant he had to go. Him leaving meant that I had to tighten the belt and survive on one income. If your current income is not enough for you to survive, you need to make more choices to increase your income, downsize your lifestyle, and survive with what you make. Some of our best work comes as a result of emergency situations. We (women) are at our best under pressure. Do what our grannies, big mamas and nanas have been doing since before we were born; take what you have and "make it enough".

Love on the rebound Whatever you do, refuse to get into another relationship immediately. Speaking from the heart; until you understand what happened in your first relationship, the chances that you will paint yourself into the same corner are a reality. Go out and meet guys; by all means, do not stay in the house wearing black. Be leery of quickly developing long-term relationships, that is what you are used to. Take my earlier advice and truly use this time to love and rebuild yourself.

If only I t is only natural for you to replay what happened in your relationship a thousand times. Replaying the relationship for the purposes of ensuring you don't make the same mistakes, miss the same signs, walk around blindly the next time, is fine. Replaying the relationship in order to blame yourself or your husband for what happened is detrimental to your health and well-being. Another cliché here is "all things happen for a reason". Look for the bright spot in the situation, and if you can't see one now keep looking. *Create* a bright spot. The bright spot for me was my kids. Had I never been with him, would I have these same kids? Also, because of my relationship with him, I moved to Houston, Texas. All of my wonderful friends and colleagues in Houston would not have my sunshine to bless them everyday, had I never been with my ex. Do you see the dominos? Don't regret the choices you make. They all impact your life is some shape, form, or fashion. Because you can't control other people, only yourself, don't beat yourself up because this relationship didn't work. Sometimes people simply outgrow each other. Sometimes you were never meant to be together in the first place.

Re-build you Physically, mentally, and financially. When you are with someone for so long, it is impossible not to lose some of yourself. I was with the same man for over seventeen years. In all of that time I have to admit that I lost some of me. This is your opportunity to explore what you like to do without compromise. Drink what you want to drink without influence. Go where you want to go without asking. Bask in this freedom. Use this time to rebuild your brand. Your brand is important. Single girls were told the same thing in their chapter. Use this time to explore what improves your happiness quotient. Live your life. If that means you happen to be alone for now, then fine. Trust me, some dude is going to see you happily living life from afar and beg to join your party of one. Who knows, maybe this is the person you were destined to be with all along? You may have just needed to make some pit stops on your journey to your soul mate.

To my Mommy Girlfriends....

I am woman! I am invincible! I am pooped! ~Author Unknown

Women with kids (yours or someone else's)

If this is not you, support your girlfriends with kids. It is truly one of those things that you have to experience to understand. Be there for her, and understand what it takes to bring another life into the world and be responsible for it.

If this is you my prayers are with you. Read on and allow me to share with you some of the things I have uncovered as I contribute to the next generation.

Positive –

- ✓ Kids are the light of your life

Opportunity –

- ✓ Preparing your kids for the future
- ✓ Kids rule the roost
- ✓ You come last - Do-it-all syndrome

Harnessing your Mommy Girl! Power

Of all of these chapters this was the hardest to write. Every word I wrote seemed like an act of betrayal to my babies, whom I love so dearly. However, I love you too, sister. Sharing this revelation was the best way for me to prove my love to you. Besides, these kids don't even care sometimes. As long as they are not impacted by what is going on in my world, they are fine. It is me who must be most concerned about putting *me* first. Breathe deeply with me, and take this next step towards finding you.

And in last place... you! I recently read a book where the author had a person in the story reflect back to the day they had their first child. The feeling they got when they held the child in their arms for the first time. This, along with many other first memories, is what guides us as parents to be prepared to put it all on the line for our kids. In my interactions with other women I have learned that this is not always what is most fair for us. Keep in mind, they do leave. When they leave you have to be prepared to live your life with limited access to them. I am not saying make decisions without regards for your children. What I am saying is don't lose touch with you and your plans for the future. Even if you don't allow your personal needs to supersede the needs of your children, realize the needs are there, and take great pains to protect and fulfill those needs. Allow me to share a personal example (You really don't have a choice, since I am the writer). For years I was out of shape and overweight. My excuse was I didn't have the time to exercise, eat right, or count calories. I was too busy taking care of my kids. One day I woke up. Now I am on the right path. The kids don't know the difference, but I do. Besides, maybe I was just being lazy and making excuses?

Head Woman in Charge Some things just have to be said. We have all seen children while we are out, who disrespect their parents. We must get a handle on this. At some point, discipline must become the focal point of our families. Whether you are a single mother, or a mother with support around you, we should all demand the respect that we were required to deliver in our own childhoods. I know everyone doesn't subscribe to corporal punishment (aka whooping their behinds). Whatever your form of discipline you believe in, make sure it is levied timely and consistently. What is cute when they are two is definitely hell when they are twelve. Invest in your children. Not just for iPods, iPads and cellphones, but for etiquette, manners, courtesy, and discipline. We have worked hard for what they have. Don't hesitate to tell them or show them where we all came from, and who had to sacrifice to get us here. They shouldn't for one minute take it for granted, and we should make sure we don't allow them to forget. I would rather spend 10,000 now to send you to boot camp for kids, than spend 100,000 later to bond you out of jail. Do what you can, with what you have now; before it's too late.

When I grow up Helping kids prepare for the future is a delicate balance. Parents are sometimes pushing kids towards the future earlier and earlier. Five year olds are in beauty pageants wearing makeup. Parents on a Pop Warner football fields fighting over a child's game. Some of us have sown so much hope into our children at such an early age, that we forget that they are just children. At the same time some of us are failing to take the time to talk to our children about drugs, teenage pregnancy, and how the decisions you make today, heavily impact your tomorrow. I don't think enough can be said about getting your kids ready to compete in today's world. The bible tells a story of burying talents. We can be guilty of allowing our kids to bury theirs, or tapping into our kids' talents too early. Allowing them to bloom while restraining our own need to see them succeed is a delicate balance.

Be Honest about where you stand Take time to evaluate the following: Are you overly aggressive in the planning of your children's activities for the future? Are you overly lenient with your children's respect for finances, sacrifices, and courtesy? Do you bypass your own needs to support the ever-growing needs of your family? Whatever your answers, commit to documenting the outcome of these answers and the steps needed to make immediate improvements.

Research what help is available for you If you feel your children are not on a path to success, admit it and get some help (Trust you are not alone). Resources exist to help us with the balance and to help them be the best they can be. Use them.

Sit down and talk to your family about your findings Whatever path you decide to pursue next, it is mandatory that you enlist the help of your family. As with all sales, if you approach it from the 'I' perspective it is doubtful you will get the support you need. Approach it instead from the perspective that you are making this change to better their lives. Remember that change is not immediate. Rome was not built in a day and your family was not spoiled in one day. It takes time for people to adjust to change. You must be the one consistent factor. Commit to day over day improvement and journal your results. Celebrate small successes, which will lead to big future impacts over time. You can only change yourself and expect for others around you to follow as a result.

Learn to say no This is surprisingly easy as you embrace the concept. Just think about it for a minute. If the kids ask you to support last minute activities often and your answer is always yes, then in their minds it is ok for them to ask you at the last minute. If at any point you say no, and explain why, then the next time they may just plan their activities a little better. This also works with people in the world. We have all been in positions where we were invited, asked, or recruited to support at the last minute. At one point I always said yes. Now I say no, not just to be uncooperative or to be mean. If completing the task will truly leave you stretched, politely decline. Let them know that had you known in advance you would have been happy to complete the tasks; however, unfortunately you have a prior commitment. Trust me that the world will not end because you cannot cook eighty cupcakes with less then 24 hours notice. The world will adjust to suit your priorities, and you may find yourself getting more respect for your time and more advance notice from those who need you.

TO MY TROPHY GIRLFRIENDS....

Most women are one man away from welfare. ~Gloria Steinem

Women whose husband is the primary or only breadwinner (I'm not talking slices here, I'm talking loaves)

If this is not you, encourage your trophy girlfriends to always think of tomorrow and to always have a backup plan if their marriage were to fail or if their breadwinner suddenly stopped bringing home the bread.

If this is you be honest about our current situation and your future. Be hesitant to tie your ability to live successfully to anyone else. Read on and take back your power.

Positive –

- ✓ Access to finances

Opportunity –

- ✓ What are you contributing to you?

HARNESSING YOUR TROPHY GIRL! POWER

Hollywood is taking advantage of what used to be taboo; Trophy wives. What started as Desperate

Housewives, and has morphed quickly into real housewives (pick your region), basketball wives, and Love and Hip Hop are all what was formerly known as trophy wives. If this is you, I am glad to have you here learning more about how to build your power. If this is one of your girls, share this with her. This may just be the best gift money *can't* buy!

Money can't buy me love I think many women fall into the trap of thinking that their man's money is their money. Well it is while you are there. What happens when he trades you in for a newer, younger model? While we all hate facing the potential truth, the fact remains that we never know, until it is too late. Those being said, enjoy the life, but ensure you protect tomorrow.

Make hay while the sun shines For this girl, access to personal finances are an obvious benefit. It is also one of the potential downfalls if the mate is to have a sudden change of heart. To that point you should keep a nest egg. In the Married Girl! Power section I talk of women who have nest eggs substantial enough to maintain their lifestyle for years to come if things were to change. You are no exception. Because you have the access to finances to make this happen, failure to do so is an egregious error on your part. Besides, with the stock market and other financial indicators being so volatile, your rainy day fund may be what saves your family from financial ruin one day.

Hone your skills Because you have access to finances, your ability to do what you love to do is easily achievable. When you love what you do, is it really work? If you love to plan parties then start your party planning business. Enlist your friends and your husbands' business partners as clients. Do it now. If at any point your husband is no longer your husband, you have the business contacts you need to continue your path to success. There are many relationships with no business need that are severed due to a breakup. Use your contacts now, before there is a chance of you being ostracized.

Create your own identity Power couples fascinate me. Especially those power couples in which the wife takes the husbands accomplishments and weaves them to create accomplishments of her own. It is true of many of our past presidents. We can just as easily remember Hilary as Bill, Barbara as George. And Michelle is performing quite nicely and is easily recognizable as her own person. Are you your own person, or are you just your husband's wife?

To my Designer Girlfriends....

Advertisers in general bare a large part of the responsibility for the deep feelings of inadequacy that drive women to psychiatrists, pills, or the bottle.
~Marya Mannes, *But Will It Sell?* 1964

Women who take pride in designer labels over future endeavors, or spend to look good now, as opposed to investing in the future

If this is not you, I have yet to meet you. We all spend a little too much trying to look good and impress the next person.

If this is you make a commitment with your girlfriends that going forward you will spend less on looking good and more on feeling good.

Positive –

✓ You take care of you

Opportunity –

✓ Finances

✓ Focus on the future and future goals

✓ Self esteem

HARNESSING YOUR DESIGNER GIRL! POWER

My own self deception didn't include present company in this chapter initially. That's right. I said "I am not a designer girl". Since purchasing thousand dollar handbags and three hundred sunglasses is not what I do, then I am not a designer girl. Oh, but wait! The truth is so important. Keeping it real cannot be denied. Whether your designer is Sam Walton (Wal-Mart) or Gucci, the risk here is the same. Retail therapy (shopping) is dangerous to our future. Most of us simply have too much and are living far above our means. Some are failing to take care of business first, and putting our futures (and families) in jeopardy. While this book encourages us to take care of ourselves, amassing mountains of credit card debt is not the way to do it. Owing everyone (and their mama) does not take care of you. It is a one way ticket to dodging bill collectors, robbing Peter to pay Paul, and provides negative impacts to your future happiness.

Shop 'til you drop A couple of years ago advertisers had us all living like the Jefferson's after they moved up. What we couldn't afford to pay cash for, we charged. Only when the economy shook under our feet like a Force 10 earthquake on the Richter scale did we wake up. For some of us it was too late. Our creditors, (the same ones who begged us to take more and more credit) were unforgiving when we lost jobs, companies downsized, and many families were forced into single or no incomes. Now what? We return to the ways of our ancestors. We protect our dollars.

Cash and CARRY It's no wonder we lost our way. Advertisers had to work really hard to pull that off. After all, I grew up listening to sayings like "a penny saved is a penny earned", and "waste not want not". My big mama squeezed a dollar so hard that the dead president would holler (she used to say that too)! We need to re-learn what our grannies taught us. Buy only what you need. Use everything, waste little, if anything. Buy re-sale when you have the chance, after all, it's new to you. Keep some money in your mattress for emergencies. Pay cash for everything but cars and houses; and do your best to pay them off quickly. Suzie Orman, Dave Ramsey, and David Bach are all outstanding financial advisors that have any number of books available to help you re-educate yourself. As the matriarch of your family you cannot afford to let the mall threaten the financial future of your family. You can't live in that Louie V bag and those Christian Leboutin's won't look attractive when you are walking everywhere because your car has been repossessed.

The reason for it all. Take a long, hard look at why we allow retail therapy to control our lives. Who are we getting dressed for? If you think about it, men couldn't care less what you have on, as long as it looks good. In some cases they don't even care about that as long as what is *in it* looks good. We have all seen dudes try to date a woman whose outfit came from Wal-mart (for all we know) and we think to ourselves, why? It's because he doesn't care. Most women get dressed for other women. After all, it is other women that will know that a bracelet you are wearing is from Tiffany's, that your sunglasses are Chanel, and that your shoes cost a small paycheck. Let's please stop trying to impress each other at the risk of our financial futures. A new outfit does not make you feel good about you. Eventually you have to take it off. The challenge is for you to look deep into yourself and decide what will truly improve your happiness quotient and then go for it. Many will witness that they feel better with thirty grand in the bank versus thirty grand worth of debt but its your choice.

Live within your means Complete an honest assessment of your family's financial situation. Within that assessment start to track how much outstanding debt you have. Make a commitment to limit personal spending until you have reduced fifty percent of your debt. Even then, provide yourself with a limit as to how much you will spend once you get there. No one arrives at their destination without a destination in mind. Chart your course to financial freedom by divorcing debt and getting a separation from retail.

Get help Use the resources I mentioned earlier or get free tips on the web to get you started. There is no reason for you to spend money to save money, but I do believe in paying authors for their work. Let this be the last fifteen to twenty dollars you spend for a while, unless you are investing in your future. Find a guru who appeals to you, write your plan on paper, and get started. Procrastination is a dream killer, so don't wait to get started.

Pay off debt Work to build your reserve. If you skip the get help option above, then this section is for you. To say simply pay off your debt and make sure you have emergency funds in the bank. Cut up credit cards and avoid stores. Dave Ramsey has an outstanding debt reduction plan called the *snowball effect*. Look him up and try it out. It has helped me go from thirty credit cards to fifteen in less than a year. My goal is to be debt free by the time you read this. Take that MasterCard!

Take your friends with you to counseling instead of the mall The best gift and the most promising support system you can have in this endeavor is your friends and family. If you don't enlist the help of your support group then you will continue to get invitations to burn down the mall (and burn up your credit). Once you and your friends have seen the light, then there is less competition within your inner circle to show up as the best dressed. Your talk then becomes the award for looking the best and spending the least, if anything. Your family will think it's a game to clip coupons and to watch the bank account grow with the money you have saved. Use that money to take a family vacation. Spend money on experiences and not things. No-one is asking you to live like a pauper. Just to buy what you can afford, to improve your happiness.

When I see the elaborate study and ingenuity displayed by women in the pursuit of trifles, I feel no doubt of their capacity for the most Herculean undertakings. ~Julia Ward Howe

TO MY PARTY GIRLFRIENDS....

I see my body as an instrument, rather than an ornament. ~Alanis Morissette, quoted in *Reader's Digest*, March 2000

Girls who party multiple nights a week, without clear life goals or direction

If this is not you, then at some point you have probably been here. Work to give your party girl friend some positive outings and help you to understand the impacts of her party lifestyle.

If this is you realize that there is more to life than parties and going out. You can truly enjoy life when your life is balanced. Read on and be encouraged to keep enjoying life.

Positive –

- ✓ Sexual freedom
- ✓ Living life

Opportunity –

- ✓ Safety
- ✓ STD's
- ✓ Priorities and goal setting

HARNESSING YOUR PARTY GIRL! POWER

Leave it to Hollywood to glamorize anything. Now they have shows about NBA, NFL, and Rapper's wives. I will tell you just like I tell my kids. My son has a one in a million shot at the NBA. If that is the case then females have a one in a million shot at marrying, or having a baby by a famous dude. Maybe that is not your thing and you just love to party. Living life is one thing, priorities are another. The faster you get your priorities in order and learn to balance the need to have fun, with the necessity of having and following a game plan, then the faster you win in the game of life. Don't be fifty or sixty and still working at a job you hate, because you spent your prime years partying every night. Read on party girl!

All play and no work Better yet, party at work. Balance is the key here. It is not suggested that you party 24 hours a day, nor is it suggested that you work 24 hours a day. Priorities must rule the day. That means you must have clear goals and direction before you set out to take the party scene by storm. That also means that your goals and direction should not include marrying into money. We all know this is a temporary situation. Take advantage of the skills you have and cultivate them to get to the next level.

The power of women We can control this Aids epidemic. And it starts with every woman. We all have the power to say no. We have the power to say, "Wrap it up... twice". We have the power to be sexually discriminate. Don't get me wrong. I am close to the biggest freak in the room, and have had my fair share of sexual partners. When I was younger, the worse you could get was something that bit or burned. This stuff now will kill you *and* your unborn children. Choose to buy some batteries and take our time before we decide to have sex.

Is it worth the risk We have all known chicks that meet a dude and go home with them the first night. Will I lie and say I haven't? No. But history (and television) teaches us some things. One hundred 'Criminal Minds' episodes later I refuse to go any place that wasn't chosen by me and that at least ten people I know, know where I am and who I am with. Get smart. Let the dude see you taking his license plate number and texting it to your girls. GPS this fools address. There is too much technology available nowadays for us to continue to live in the dark.

Do what you love As a true party girl there are a myriad of careers that will allow you to be successful while still clinging to the party scene. If you love the night life, what about being a party planner? Love to shop, try being a personal shopper for the stars. Your future is up to you. Don't allow lack of self esteem to turn you into a groupie. There is room for everyone at the show, including you. Play your part. Continue to live life to the fullest, but keep the future in mind. The future is where we are headed and we can't just ignore it and trust that it will take care of itself.

One does not have to sleep with, or even touch, someone who has paid for your meal. All those obligations are hereby rendered null and void, and any man who doesn't think so needs a quick jab in the kidney. ~Cynthia Heimel, *Sex Tips for Girls*, 1983

TO MY (PLUS SIZED) GIRLFRIENDS ...

I am beautiful as I am. I am the shape that was gifted. My breasts are no longer perky and upright like when I was a teenager. My hips are wider than that of a fashion models. For this I am glad, for these are the signs of a life lived. ~Cindy Olsen, co-owner of The Body Objective

Girls, big beautiful women, more to love, just need to lose ten pounds or any other woman not satisfied with her size or shape (I refuse to put a pound range)

If this is not you, realize that the big girl in your life is not big because she chose to be. There are many factors that cause us to be overweight. Support the big girl in your life and let her know that you love her regardless. Don't preach about eating right, but instead talk about being healthy if you have to talk about anything. Most of us know what to do, it is just having the will power and energy to do it.

If this is you love yourself for who you are and the people around you will too. If you are upset about your size work to change it; however don't let it take over the beauty you have inside.

Positive –

- ✓ You are a *real* woman

Opportunity –

✓ Health issues

✓ Self esteem can be a critical issue, impacting how you view yourself and therefore, impacting how you allow others to treat you.

HARNESSING YOUR BIG GIRL! POWER

I am many of the women in this book... or have been at some point in my life. Of these many women I am now, and continue to fight the battle of the bulge. Weight loss is critical for a healthier you. But at the same time we must refuse to be unhappy with our present selves. For years I was so unhappy that I believe I truly stopped even trying to lose weight. Shame on me! If you can adopt one good habit year over year, this contributes to weight loss over time. Rome wasn't built in a day, and I damn sure didn't get fat eating one misplaced chicken wing or slice of pizza. So let's discuss ways to love you while staying on the road to less you to love.

Get over the media If we listened to Vogue and Cosmo everyone would be a size five...not! I have known women who were as thin as supermodels in the past who were not happy, I now know that thin is not the road to bliss. As I have stated in many sections of this book, the key to bliss is balance. I may have a taste for pizza, but the key is not to eat the whole damn pie. We have to love ourselves enough to make good choices and throw a middle finger in Hollywood's direction for even suggesting that all of us should be paper thin! Beauty is in the eye of the beholder. We big girls need to surround ourselves with people who love us for who we are (and that can carry us in the case of an emergency, or at least phone for help!).

A healthy you For many years I was plagued with denial. Depression, self esteem and many personal issues kept me from pursuing the path to weight loss. An epiphany at forty changed my outlook and now I am on the road. I have not arrived at the destination, but I am on the road to improve my health daily. Will you join me? We may be passed by others on this road, but slow and steady wins the race. Again, Rome wasn't built in a day. And this fat suit that I am carrying was not either. But it's me at any rate and I love me. Love yourself!

Commit to working a plan, any plan What I have noticed about my thin partners is that they don't subscribe to one plan. They bounce around plans like a ping pong ball. This does not mean they are fickle. What this means is that they are constantly trying something new. And this is what we have to do. I have tried Weight Watchers, Atkins, South Beach, Slim Fast, and I always lose. But when I stop trying, I gain it back. So the answer is to never stop trying. If you get bored with one plan, start another. Some of them cost money. But at the end of the day we would have spent the money on burgers and shakes anyway, why not spend on something worthwhile like our health? If the only consequence of being heavy was some people may not like it, then I truly would not care. But let's face it, there are too many studies that show obesity and carrying extra weight impacts our one-way ticket to life. Since I want to stay longer, I must continue to try to be a better (and fitter), me.

We fall down Eating is a habit. Unlike some addictions that are privately conducted in the closet, everywhere you go there is a reason for you to feed your habit. My Weight Watchers instructor once told me this. She said that people gain weight for Thanksgiving. But Thanksgiving is a holiday. Holi**day**! One day. Not the entire week. Not from Thursday through Sunday. It is only one day. If we ate healthy for the rest of the year, then the holidays wouldn't matter. If we eat like we are crazy for the holiday, then the next day we need to climb our crazy behinds back on the wagon. We fall down, but we get up. That's what Donnie MClurkin said and that's what we *must* subscribe to.

Gimmicks and quick weight loss diets Please forgive me this one commercial. Throughout this diatribe I have attempted to reserve many opinions and stick with experiences and facts. In this case I must say that I don't subscribe to the quick weight loss scams. This includes going under the knife to lose weight. We all know someone who has had a poor experience under the knife. Willpower, exercise, and self love would have served the same purpose. Sure, it may have taken more time, but the end results are worth it. Ditch the gimmicks, take a walk, and eat some fruit and salads. If, at the end of the day, you feel the risks of going under the knife are worth it, then do what you have to do. Do something to be healthier sister. I love you. You must love you too!

Big and Unhappy We all have our personal self esteem issues, and since I happen to be a big girl, I know that at times the fact that I am big drives me to eat even more! Don't allow your pity party to continue to be your downfall. Use that energy to get up and go to the gym. Join some exercise classes where you may just meet people who will accept you for you and who you have something in common with. When you go to the gym, every person there, whether big or small, is there with one goal in mind... to be healthier!

TO MY GIRLFRIENDS WHO LOVE THE ENVIRONMENT (ALL OF US)....

I would feel more optimistic about a bright future for man if he spent less time proving that he can outwit Nature and more time tasting her sweetness and respecting her seniority. - E. B. White

All Girls who love the environment (and since we all love to breath, this is all of us)

If this is not you, it should be. Think about the impacts we have each day to the world around us, and commit to leaving the world better than we found it.

If this is you keep reading and look for ways to impact your girlfriends and your community.

Positive –

- ✓ It's a smaller job than you think

Opportunity –

- ✓ Focus on social issues
- ✓ Focus on community involvement

HARNESSING YOUR GREEN GIRL! POWER

What world will we leave for the next generation? Will our greed and need to have the biggest, brightest, and fastest everything cast us back to the stone ages? I should hope not. That is why I wrote the next chapter. I Can't lie to you (remember my promise to keep it real?), as I write this, my carbon foot print is the same as my shoe size; huge! I am trying and my plan to continue trying stretches for the next generation. The commitment here is that we will raise awareness, try harder to conserve, waste less, and protect our world more. An attempt at anything goes further than no attempt at all. So come with me sister, to a place where we may have to make some sacrifices (sorry, I am holding on to the toilet paper) in order for us to leave a better world.

It's not easy being Green Who should be blamed for the world's current state? It's easy to blame the manufacturers and these big companies who put out products that are simply wasteful. But at some point we must point the finger back at ourselves for easily accepting what's easy. After all, being green takes some effort, and although the push for saving the environment makes some things easier, it still takes time and energy to go green. But we must do it anyway. We were given a gift and it is sacrilegious to take that gift for granted. We have to say to ourselves, "how much am I willing to give?" And if we all give a little, chances are things will get easier and improvement will be seen.

It's not cute being Green We have all seen the hybrid cars. And I just told you I am a big girl. In my mind, the two don't mesh! Real Talk. I don't want to be calling for help every morning just to pry myself out of the car. However, manufacturers are getting better, and more options are becoming available. And maybe, just maybe, I don't have to get rid of the town car yet. What are some changes that I can make that are seamless? Freezing food so it doesn't waste? Avoiding Styrofoam containers? Recycling at home? Using earth friendly light bulbs and paper products? Those are just a few examples. And when I leave the house you don't know that I have on clothes and jewelry that came from a thrift store. Or that the shoes I have on, while fly, were made by an environmentally friendly company. So maybe, just maybe, as we all shift towards being green, and making green choices, it becomes even better looking and easier for us to keep it going.

Be green anyway Take small (but green) steps towards getting this earth back on track. I mentioned a few of them above. Want to even further your impact? Get your girlfriends involved. Girl! Power is nothing to sneeze at. Especially when we multiply that power by five, ten or twenty; the impact becomes phenomenal. Start a green girl night out, where you guys discuss ways of making green easy. Serve green drinks in recycled cups. Eat organically grown salads, or Asian ribs from animals that are steroid free. Make it fun. But do something. When it's all said and done we can take pride in knowing that we were not the generation that changed the world forever, for the worse!

TO MY SILVER GIRLFRIENDS....

A man has every season while a woman only has the right to spring. ~Jane Fonda

Dedicated to my mom and all of the silver foxes out there. (I refuse to put an age range here)

If this is not you, look for the silver girlfriends in your circle. Don't miss the chance to make them feel valuable and even tapping into their value for you and your girlfriends.

If this is you God has you here for a reason. Look for ways to support your family and to have your family support your dreams.

Positive –

- ✓ God ain't done with you yet!

Opportunity –

- ✓ Focus on the future

- ✓ Retirement Savings

HARNESSING YOUR SILVER GIRL! POWER

I call my mom Granny simply because my kids do. If I could send this book back in time, my mom would be a different woman. It is not too late for me to make an impact on my favorite silver fox; my mom is brilliant, loving, wonderful, and smart. There's just one problem; she doesn't know it. Not sure how the generation before us, who instilled so much self love and self esteem in us missed it for themselves. So here is a chance to give back. Make sure your mom reads this. And if she is no longer with us, share this with another silver fox. They will be glad you did.

There is still much to share Don't think because you are up in years that you have contributed all you can. There is an entire generation of women who need you! From the teens who are struggling to find love, to the women my age who no longer have their mothers, we need you. We need your life experiences, your intelligence and we flat out need your love. Reach out and give it to us. We may not be a hundred percent accepting initially, because we hear so much criticism around us, but when we realize your true intentions we will be accepting. God is not done with you yet! Find purpose in what you are here to do, and who needs you to help them over the wall.

Tired of being Tired Baby Boomers missed the mark on saving for retirement. And social security is tripping. My advice is to find what you like to do and make a part-time (or full-time) career of it. There is an entire world out there that is begging you to give us your best. My mom likes to sew. Not only does she like to do it, but she is great at it. Why work for someone when you can work for *you*, doing what *you* love. It's not too late to get up, get out, and make some extra income that will allow you to stop punching clocks within the next few years.

No time to waste Evaluate and get moving. As I have asked the other Girls! in this book, find out what you are good at and do it. If you have had a dream for the last few years, this is your chance. If you need some help there many resources around to help you off to a great start. Enlist the help of your family members, children, nieces, nephews, grandchildren. This is your legacy and we will be happy to carry it forward for you. Don't miss the opportunity to get started.

GIRL! POWER DISCUSSION QUESTIONS

Now that you have read the book I want to give you a jump start in talking about this with your girlfriends. You can use each one of these questions to jumpstart conversation the next time you have a Girl! Power gathering. You don't have to discuss these all at once, but they are great conversation starters. Be truthful to each other while discussing, and be truthful to yourself when answering.

1. In reading Real Girl Power, which girl do you feel you related to more? Did you relate to more than one girl in the book?

2. After reading the different girl types. Do you think you feel that every girl type was represented well in the book? If not what girl type would you add to the book?

3. Do you feel that any one girl type has more obstacles than the others? If so who and why?

4. Why as women, do we allow obstacles (men, circumstances, and other obstacles) prevent us from pursuing our dreams?

5. Men do not allow distractions to interfere with their goals. Why do we? Which girl type in the book do you feel would be the least likely to allow herself to be distracted from her goals.

6. What do you do to keep yourself from getting complacent? Do you have a confidant, mentor, or that one friend that will say hey "you tripping girl"?

7. Take a moment to look at the different girl types again. Which girl type is most like your best or close friend and why? What can you do to be more supportive of her and her dreams.

8. As women we are prone to taking on too much. We are usually moving at such a warp speed, we seldom pause to take a breath. Which girl type would you say is the most likely to say that "any happiness you get, you have to make it yourself"?

9. In closing, think of your girl type. What is the lasting impression she left on you?

10. Each girl type is unique in her own way. Feel confident in you. Take the time to go around and let each girl friend speak on the power they bring to the group.

    Encourage each other to look for the positive and to embrace the passion that will take us all to the next level.

Special thanks to my Diva Girlfriend Alisa Granberry for her help with the discussion questions. You are a bad chick!

GIRL! POWER PARTY IDEAS

GREEN GIRL PARTY

Remember our commitment to keeping it green? Below are some suggestions for having a "green girl" party. Remember we are to take our men with us on this journey so they are definitely invited.

1. CHOOSE A DATE AND TIME THAT WORKS FOR YOUR GIRLS
2. INVITE EVERYONE AND TELL THEM UP FRONT IT IS A GREEN GIRL PARTY, SEND THE INVITE ELECTRONICALLY OR ON ENVIRONMENTALLY FRIENDLY PAPER.
3. ASK EACH OF YOUR GUESTS TO BRING ONE EASY TO IMPLEMENT IDEA THAT WILL HELP TO PROTECT THE ENVIRONMENT AND/OR SAVE ENERGY
4. SERVE GREEN COCKTAILS, BEER IN GREEN BOTTLES, AND ORGANICALLY GROWN FOOD (YOU CAN ALSO ASK YOUR GUESTS TO BRING ONE GREEN MENU ITEM OR BEVERAGE)
5. ALLOW EACH GUESTS 2 OR 3 MINUTES TO DISCUSS THEIR IDEA
6. PLAY MUSIC, PLAY CARDS, HAVE FUN, YOU DON'T HAVE TO STAY GREEN THE ENTIRE PARTY. THE POINT IS TO KICK OFF YOUR PARTY BY WORKING TO IMPROVE OUR WORLD AND TO MAKE CONSERVATION A FOCUS, IF ONLY FOR AN HOUR.

DESIGNER GIRL PARTY

Let's just face it. We all probably shop too much for current economic trends. Below are some ideas to help you and your girlfriends by taking some of the focus away from retail therapy and put the focus back on future investments.

1. CHOOSE A DATE AND TIME THAT WORKS FOR YOUR GIRLS
2. INVITE EVERYONE AND TELL THEM UP FRONT IT IS A DESIGNER GIRL PARTY
3. ASK EACH OF YOUR GUESTS TO COME PREPARED TO SHARE THE STORY OF ONE HIGH DOLLAR PURCHASE THAT THEY REGRET AND WHAT THEY COULD HAVE DONE DIFFERENTLY WITH THAT MONEY
4. SERVE INEXPESIVE COCKTAILS THAT COULD BE COMPARED TO PRICIER BRANDS
5. ALLOW EACH GUESTS 2 OR 3 MINUTES TO DISCUSS THEIR PURCHASE AND WHAT THEY WILL DO DIFFERENTLY GOING FORWARD
6. GET A COMMITMENT FROM EACH GUEST AS TO WHAT THEY WILL DO THE NEXT TIME THEY FEEL LIKE BURNING DOWN THE MALL
7. PLAY MUSIC, PLAY CARDS, AND ENJOY EACH OTHER. THIS IS NOT PUNISHMENT, THIS IS GROWTH. FOR YOURSELF AND FOR YOUR GIRLS.

CARD CUTTING PARTY

As we work to return to cash and carry, and reduce some of our stress by reducing some of our debt, a card cutting party is a great symbolic way to start our journey.

1. CHOOSE A DATE AND TIME THAT WORKS FOR YOUR GIRLS
2. INVITE EVERYONE AND TELL THEM UP FRONT IT IS A CARD CUTTING PARTY
3. ASK EACH OF YOUR GUESTS TO COME PREPARED WITH ONE OR SEVERAL CREDIT CARDS THAT THEY WOULD LIKE TO "CUT UP" AND COMMIT TO PAYING OFF AND/OR NOT USING ANY MORE UNTIL PAID OFF
4. SERVE INEXPESIVE COCKTAILS THAT COULD BE COMPARED TO PRICIER BRANDS
5. ALLOW EACH GUESTS 2 OR 3 MINUTES TO DISCUSS THEIR CURRENT CARD SITUATION AND CELEBRATE AS EACH CARD IS CUT
6. GET A COMMITMENT FROM EACH GUEST AS TO HOW THEY WILL PREVENT CREDIT CARD DEBT IN THE FUTURE.
7. PLAY MUSIC, PLAY CARDS, AND ENJOY EACH OTHER. THIS IS NOT PUNISHMENT, THIS IS GROWTH. FOR YOURSELF AND FOR YOUR GIRLS.

AND SO ON....

Now that you get the idea I won't bore you with the details. After all, I am sure you have an imagination too. Here are some other ideas for Girl! Power parties, give them your own twist, make them your own, and come up with other ideas to add to these.

FINANCIAL FOCUS PARTY

Have each girl in the group bring tips on how to save money, or a book to exchange to help others with their finances.

WEIGHT LOSS/HEALTHY EATING PARTY

Plan a party that includes tips on healthy eating and/or weight loss. If everyone agrees you can even create a "pot" of money and weigh in at each meeting to see who has lost the most % to goal of weight and determine who wins the money. Remember not to put anyone on the spot and perhaps even go on the honor system if every is not comfortable with group weigh in. Have the meeting at a gym, outside, at a

Coupon Clipping Party

Have everyone bring several weeks of coupons from the Sunday paper and spend time clipping the coupons and sharing the coupons with each other. Guest can talk about how to multiply coupon savings, and you can even watch shows or exchange books on making coupons work for your family. There are coupon organizers available at most dollar stores that the host can provide to the guest, or have each guest bring their own.

Strength in Numbers Party

Have each guests invite a guest that is new to the group, but can assist the group in a professional capacity. Invite lawyers, accountants, and even day care professionals. The point is to leverage one another's contacts to make the group even stronger. Also the contacts who are invited get a chance to learn about the needs of the different guest. Who knows, they may need one of your services, in which case a win-win is created.

Study Party

Invite all of your classmates over for cocktails (coffee) and study time. Invite the guys too as many of them are great in assisting with school work.

TUTOR PARTY

Determine the ages of the children within your group. Bring all of the children together for "tutor" time. You can either split the cost of a "tutor" for the group, or hire one of the groups' older children who are currently in college and may need the extra cash. You can have this party during the week and have each girl in the group chip in items towards the evening meal.

SILVER GIRL PARTY

Invite your moms, and other silver girls who are active in the community to your party to discuss their life experiences. This is a great chance to not only learn from the, but to also make them feel valued for the contributions they have made to our current standard of living. Remember these are the ladies who marched on Washington, boycotted buses, and burned bras for our equality.

MOMMY GIRL PARTY

Have a night where you come together just to talk about your children. Discuss the obstacles you are having including behavioral issues and be prepared to share what you did to overcome and the resources that are available to assist.

Girl! Power Get Away

Once or twice a year if you can, well in advance, plan a get away with just you and the girls. You can have a girl power party to plan it. Invite travel agents who are willing to work with your budgets and can help with good ideas on where to go. If the travel agent can't come in person, perhaps they are available by phone. Whatever it takes to make these annual getaways happen, make it important.

Prayer Party

It is not secret that prayer changes things. Have a gathering where you share the things you are praying and hoping to change most, and take the opportunity to pray for each other. Commit to praying for each other for a specific period of time. Be ready to share testimonies when you have a breakthrough on what you were praying for. Give God the glory for what is sure to be an encouraging and empowering evening.

I AM PARTY

Sometimes as women we are so busy saying what we are NOT we forget to claim what we are. Have a party where you encourage your guests to write down 10 – 15 things that they wish to be as though they already have occurred. Each guest should commit to reading this list out loud each morning and evening as a positive affirmation to the change that is about to take place in their lives.

CREATE THE DREAM PARTY

Visualizing our dream is an important step in dream fulfillment. Have a party where you invite all of your guests to bring 4 or 5 old magazines. Have the host provide scissors, poster board, and glue (or have your guest bring one item each). Spend the evening discussing the dreams for your life with your friends and clipping out pictures that symbolize those dreams. If you want to lose weight cut out a picture of someone who already looks like you want to. Maybe your goal is a happy family, then cut out a picture of one. Once the board is finished explain your board so that your girl friends can help you when possible. Take the board home or to work where it can serve as a daily remember to you of your dream. The motivation should inspire you to work on your dream each day.

CLOSING THOUGHTS

4/11/11

I completed this book on 4/11/11. I was also born in November (11th month) With so many eleven's at work, I had to look up the significance of the number eleven.

Number eleven possesses the qualities of intuition, patience, honesty, sensitivity, and spirituality, and is idealistic. Others turn to people who are 'Eleven' for teaching and inspiration, and are usually uplifted by the experience.

I was moved by this because as I wrote my book, these terms describe my vision. Intuition was my guiding light as I wrote. Gut instinct told me what would help you on your journey. And that is what is captured on paper. Although I drove myself to write this book, this book is a culmination of years of patience in capturing the struggles of my sisters (all colors - don't get it twisted). I told you I would keep it real, and so honesty is not only prevalent throughout, but mandatory. I was sensitive but still tough on this journey to help you tap into your power. God is the giver of all, so my spirituality shines through. And although idealistic about the goals in this book, I have no doubts that by envisioning them, they can be captured.

This book represents teaching and inspiration and I can only hope you are uplifted by the experience. Look for more to come... God is not done with me yet!

With Love,

Your sister,

P.S. I still love you. 2nd edition October 2011

ACKNOWLEDGEMENTS

First and foremost, the strong women in my life; Deborah Patterson (my Mom), for giving me life and so much more! Addie Patterson (Big Mama) for being my kindred spirit. I get this fire from her! My aunts Maxine Patterson, Veronica Patterson, and Donna Jean "Paw Paw" Patterson.

To my career mother and father, Benita Nugent and Tommie English (Both women, long story! Trust me)

To my first and favorite mentor Cynthia Rollins I continue to pay the lessons forward.

To my sisters and girlfriends given to me by God, Tonisha Johnson, D'ambra Shuaib, Effua Mcgowan and Martha Adams. Thanks for always keeping it real with me.

To Breana Goode for keeping me looking good to the eye.

Melissa Westbury and Shabby Chic Photography for helping my spirit to shine through in photos.

HRD design for breathing life into my book covers.

Anita Davies for breathing life into the contents. Thanks for being available at all times of day and night!

To my colleagues, friends, and family! Thanks for being my support system. I could not have done it without you.

If I missed anyone, please charge it to the head and not the heart!

With much love girlfriend,

DpW October, 2011

www.ingramcontent.com/pod-product-compliance
Lightning Source LLC
Chambersburg PA
CBHW031223090426
42740CB00007B/683